Delhi

by Betsy Rathburn
Illustrated by Diego Vaisberg

T0015036

BLASTOFF!
MISSIONS

BELLWETHER MEDIA
MINNEAPOLIS, MN

Blastoff! Missions takes you on a learning adventure! Colorful illustrations and exciting narratives highlight cool facts about our world and beyond. Read the mission goals and follow the narrative to gain knowledge, build reading skills, and have fun!

Traditional Nonfiction

BLASTOFF! READERS

BLASTOFF! Beginners

BLASTOFF! DISCOVERY

BLASTOFF! MISSIONS

Narrative Nonfiction

Blastoff! Universe

MISSION GOALS

> FIND YOUR SIGHT WORDS IN THE BOOK.

> LEARN ABOUT DIFFERENT TIMES IN DELHI'S HISTORY.

> LEARN ABOUT DIFFERENT PEOPLE OR GROUPS WHO HAVE CONTROLLED DELHI.

This edition first published in 2024 by Bellwether Media, Inc.

No part of this publication may be reproduced in whole or in part without written permission of the publisher. For information regarding permission, write to Bellwether Media, Inc., Attention: Permissions Department, 6012 Blue Circle Drive, Minnetonka, MN 55343.

Library of Congress Cataloging-in-Publication Data

LC record for Delhi available at: https://lccn.loc.gov/2023044999

Editor: Christina Leaf   Designer: Andrea Schneider

Printed in the United States of America, North Mankato, MN.

This is **Blastoff Jimmy**! He is here to help you on your mission and share fun facts along the way!

Table of Contents

Welcome to Delhi!

Welcome to one of the world's biggest cities! Delhi, India, is a mix of old and new. About 33 million people live in and around the city. Let's explore its past!

Built by Many

Anangpal II

Here comes the king! Anangpal II is here to visit his new city. Those workers are finishing the **fortress**. The tall wall will protect against **invaders**!

fortress

1220

Look up! That man is calling **Muslims** to prayer.

Delhi's first Muslim ruler started this **minaret**. The new ruler Iltutmish finished it.

▶ JIMMY SAYS ◀

The minaret still stands today. It is 238 feet (72.5 meters) tall!

1640s

It is a time of wealth and growth in Delhi! Shah Jahan plans to move the **Mughal** capital here.

He funds many artistic projects. This Red Fort will use many different building styles!

Red Fort

▶ **JIMMY SAYS** ◀

Shah Jahan also built the Taj Mahal in Agra. It is one of India's most famous buildings!

Finding Freedom

rebel

1857

Rebels fight for freedom from British rule. They have taken over Delhi.

Now, British troops strike back. They are here to take back the city. Can India break free?

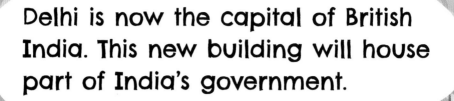

1927

Delhi is now the capital of British India. This new building will house part of India's government.

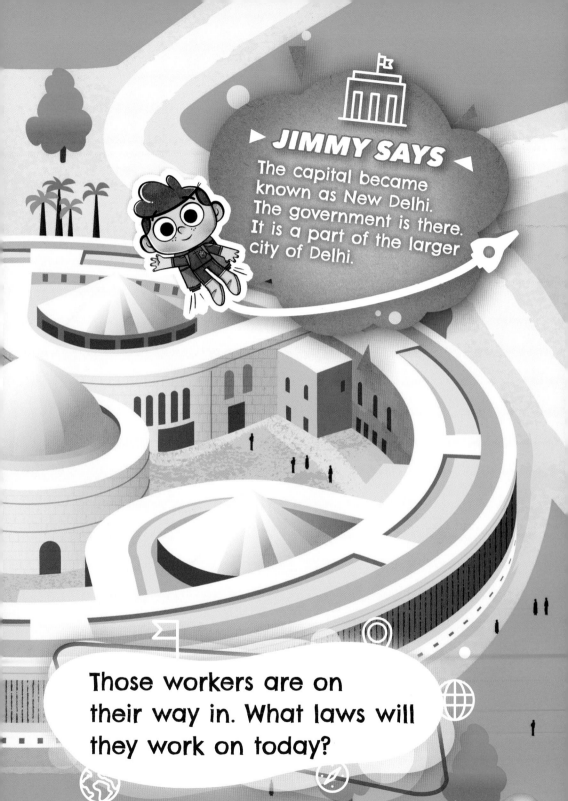

JIMMY SAYS

The capital became known as New Delhi. The government is there. It is a part of the larger city of Delhi.

Those workers are on their way in. What laws will they work on today?

India's flag

1947

This crowd is loud! People gather to celebrate in Delhi's streets. India's new **prime minister** raises the country's flag. India is finally free from British rule!

1986

Look at the new Lotus **Temple**! This building is shaped like a flower.

People of all beliefs have come to visit. All are welcome here!

Lotus Temple

The City Today

today

Buses and trains zip past **monuments** and markets. **Pedicabs** take people to cafes. Delhi grows and changes. It is always busy!

monument

pedicab

Delhi Timeline

1060 CE: Lal Kot fortress is finished by Anangpal II

1220: Soon after Muslims take control of the area, Iltutmish finishes the minaret Qutb Minar

1640s: The Red Fort is built

1857: Rebels who want freedom from British rule briefly take over Delhi

1927: The Parliament House is finished 16 years after Great Britain makes Delhi its imperial capital in India

1947: To celebrate independence, India's new prime minister raises the flag in Delhi

1986: Lotus Temple is finished

Delhi, India

Glossary

fortress–a protected place for an army

invaders–people who come from one place to take over another place

minaret–a tall tower from which a person calls Muslims to prayer

monuments–buildings or other structures built to honor something

Mughal–related to the Mughal rulers of India; the Mughals held power in India from 1526 until 1858.

Muslims–people who follow the Islamic faith; Islam is based on the teachings of the Prophet Muhammad as told to him by Allah.

pedicabs–small taxis operated with pedals

prime minister–the leader of the government in some countries

rebels–people who act against a ruler or government

temple–a building used for worship

To Learn More

AT THE LIBRARY

Chanda, Anurima. *Timelines from Indian History: From Ancient Civilizations to a Modern Democracy*. New York, N.Y.: DK Publishing, 2021.

Davies, Monika. *India*. Minneapolis, Minn.: Bellwether Media, 2023.

Markovics, Joyce. *Delhi*. New York, N.Y.: Bearport Publishing, 2018.

ON THE WEB

FACTSURFER

Factsurfer.com gives you a safe, fun way to find more information.

1. Go to www.factsurfer.com.

2. Enter "Delhi" into the search box and click 🔍.

3. Select your book cover to see a list of related content.

BEYOND THE MISSION

> WHICH PART OF DELHI'S HISTORY WOULD YOU LIKE TO VISIT? WHY?

> DESIGN A NEW BUILDING IN DELHI. WHAT DOES IT LOOK LIKE? WHAT IS IT FOR?

> WHAT DO YOU THINK DELHI WILL BE LIKE IN THE FUTURE?

Index